Lovingly Dedicated

To my wife, Kathee, and to Little David
—David

To my Mother and to Gary
—Don

WHAT YOU CAN SEE
YOU CAN BE!

You can fight a fire
If you so desire

Or do a dance
    If you take the chance

Or build a jet
    And learn to fly,
Or whatever you see
    In your mind's eye

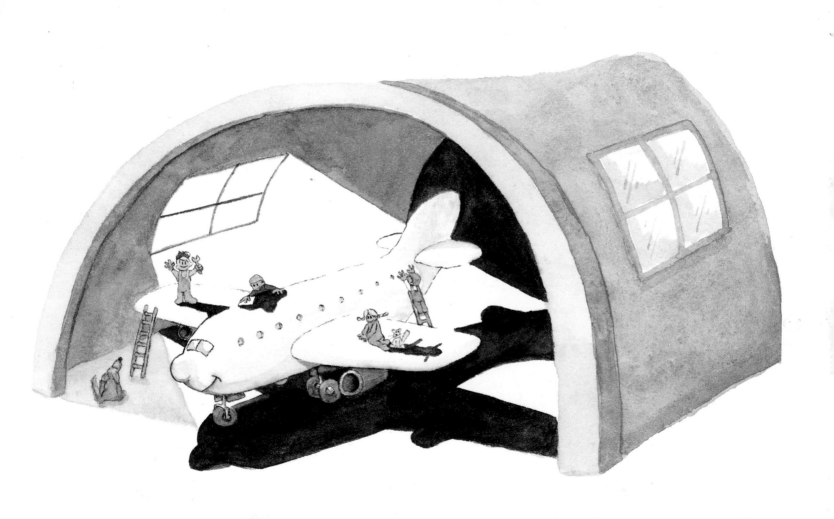

Because what you can see,
You can be!

Believe it's so
    And it's true!
It's just that easy;
    It's up to you!

Plant a seed
    Within your mind,
And it will blossom
    In due time

Because what you can see,
Can be!

It's very simple;
   Here's what to do
(Now think of something good
   Because it will come true!)

Picture yourself
  Having or being or doing
  Whatever you desire today.
Put the picture in a bubble,
  Then let it float away.

Trust that it will happen,
    Let go of it all the way;
Don't forget to say thank you,
    Then go outside and play!

Now don't you doubt
    And don't you fear
'Cause that blocks out
    What you want to hear.

Just see it and believe it,
    And claim it's already yours;
Know that it will happen,
    And <u>that</u> opens all the doors!

Remember, what you can see,
You can be!

You can picture for now

Or picture for later

For your mom or dad
Or your pet alligator!

But be careful
   In what you choose . . .
Keep your thinking positive
   And you'll never lose!

Because what you see,
Will come to be!

Knowing you can do this,
    You needn't worry or fear.
Good will always guide you
    When you're quiet enough to hear.

See the good around you
And know it will be there.
<u>Give</u> love and you'll <u>receive</u> love;
That's a promise we all share!

'Bye now — and remember
   That what you think and see
Has a wonderful way of becoming
   The person you will be.